The Weightiness of God

The Weightiness of God

Warren Hunter

Sword Ministries International
Branson, Missouri

The Weightiness of God
Published by:
Sword Ministries International
3044 Shepherd of the Hills
Exprwy Ste 649
Branson, MO 65616
ISBN 1-889816-21-3

Cover design by:
Rick Collins
Visual Candy
713-621-8472
16210 Blackhawk Blvd.
Friendswood, TX 77546

Book production by:
DB & Associates Design Group, Inc.
dba Double Blessing Productions
P.O. Box 52756, Tulsa, OK 74152
www.dbassoc.org

Printed in the United States of America.

Contents

Introduction

In the Beginning...

In the beginning God created the heavens and the earth.

And darkness [was] on the face of the deep. And the Spirit of God moved on the face of the waters.

And God said, Let there be light. And there was light.

Genesis 1:1-3 (MKJV)

The Bible says, "In the beginning God created the heaven and the earth," yet strangely enough, it doesn't say anything about God's glory. This isn't surprising, because one of the major reasons God gave Genesis 1:1 to Israel was to let them know that it was God that created the heavens and the earth. The pagan gods such as Baal, or some of the Egyptian gods, were in no way responsible for this glorious creation.

Nevertheless, if we take all of scripture into account and read between the lines, we can see *everything* that God does is fruitful or glorious, without exception. Even at creation, God's glory was no doubt present and active.

But what precisely does the word glory mean? This is a word that has been used frequently by the religious, most often with very little understanding of its meaning and origin. For this reason, I feel it's essential to begin by looking into what the glory of God really means.

Chapter 1
The Essence of Glory

Jacob and Laban

Interestingly enough, the first time that glory is mentioned specifically in the Bible is when Jacob is with his uncle, Laban.

Remember how Jacob got tricked and ended up with Laban's two daughters, both Leah and Rachel, as wives? As a result of Laban's deception, Jacob ended up having to work for his uncle several more years.

As the time of their extended agreement drew to a close, they eventually worked out a plan for Jacob's payment with the cattle. Jacob would get all the striped, speckled and spotted lambs, and Laban would keep the rest.

So he said, "What shall I give you?" And Jacob said, "You shall not give me anything. If you will do this thing for me, I will again feed and keep your flocks:

"Let me pass through all your flock today, removing from there all the speckled and spotted sheep, and all the brown ones among the lambs, and the spotted and the speckled among the goats; and these shall be my wages.

"So my righteousness will answer for me in time to come, when the subject of my wages comes before you: every one that is not speckled and spotted among the goats, and brown among the lambs, will be considered stolen, if it is with me."

And Laban said, "Oh, that it were according to your word!"

So he removed that day the male goats that were speckled and spotted, all the female goats that were speckled and spotted, every one that had some white in it, and all the brown ones among the lambs, and gave them into the hand of his sons.

Then he put three days' journey between himself and Jacob, and Jacob fed the rest of Laban's flocks.

Now Jacob took for himself rods of green poplar and of the almond and chestnut trees, peeled white strips in them, and exposed the white which was in the rods.

And the rods which he had peeled, he set before the flocks in the gutters, in the watering troughs where the flocks came to drink, so that they should conceive when they came to drink.

So the flocks conceived before the rods, and the flocks brought forth streaked, speckled, and spotted.

Then Jacob separated the lambs, and made the flocks face toward the streaked and all the brown in the flock of Laban; but he put his own flocks by themselves and did not put them with Laban's flock.

And it came to pass, whenever the stronger livestock conceived, that Jacob placed the rods before

the eyes of the livestock in the gutters, that they might conceive among the rods.

But when the flocks were feeble, he did not put them in; so the feebler were Laban's and the stronger Jacob's.

Thus the man became exceedingly prosperous, and had large flocks, female and male servants, and camels and donkeys.

Genesis 30:31-43

In order to obtain the strongest flocks, Jacob laid different types of sticks in front of them. As a result, Jacob's lambs began to breed before the water and his lambs began to be more than those belonging to Laban.

What was happening? The blessings of God were beginning to multiply in Jacob's life. He was getting weighty, prosperous and blessed.

Even Laban's sons recognized God's blessings, and they soon became jealous of Jacob's success.

And he heard the words of Laban's sons, saying, Jacob has taken away all that [was] our father's, and he has gotten all this glory from that which was our father's.

Genesis 31:1 (MKJV)

In this instance, material wealth is equated with the term *"glory."* However, the material blessings that Laban's sons could see were only physical manifestations of the glory that was on Jacob's life, a glory that had been passed down from his grandfather Abraham.

The Blessing Aspect

When God talked to Abraham, He told Abraham that He would bless those who bless him and curse those who curse him. Take a closer look and see how glory is connected to this.

"blessing I will bless you, and multiplying I will multiply your descendants as the stars of the heaven and as the sand which is on the seashore; and your descendants shall possess the gate of their enemies."

Genesis 22:17

...That year Isaac's crops were tremendous! He harvested a hundred times more grain than he planted, for the LORD blessed him.

He became a rich man, and his wealth only continued to grow.

Genesis 26:12,13 (NLT)

Here we see just a small glimpse of God's infinite power to bless. Just like the stars in the sky are too numerous to count, God's ability and willingness to bless his people is also impossible for us to measure. This is indeed a vital part of God's glory.

Nevertheless, this is an aspect of God's glory that many people miss. God's unlimited power to bless His children is an essential aspect of His glory, just like His loving kindness and mercy.

We must understand that it's all part of *the same God*. For many years, God's people have divided God up as if He were an ala carte dinner and taken only the portions that they were comfortable with. But God's glory is not something that can be divided up. God must be accepted as He is, in all of His glory and splendor. It's a grave error to accept the salvation aspect and ignore the blessing aspect.

Why is it that so many are ready to believe God will save them, but totally reject that same One who wants to bless them and increase them in all areas? I think much of this comes from a failure to understand the meaning of glory.

Weight and Splendor

It's regrettable that most people can't even begin to understand the word "glory" in and of itself. It's somewhat like other words such as grace or righteousness that people have a tendency to read over and to assign some vague religious meaning. But that is a mistake.

As we begin to explore the wide range of meanings behind this word, we find the word glory to be translated from the original Hebrew word Kabowd.

The word glory (Kabowd) in other English Bible translations is sometimes even translated as *wealth*.

One thing I found to be quite interesting is the definition of *Kabowd* in Strong's Concordance. In addition to being translated glory, and even honor, it can also mean *weight* and *splendor*.

If you consider these definitions more closely, it doesn't really seem odd that these things are listed together. When God appears on the scene there always seems to be a weightiness and splendor in the air. In fact, when one thinks of the word glory by itself, it's somewhat difficult to imagine glory in action. However, if you think of wealth, honor, heaviness and splendor you begin to get a picture of glory in operation.

God is no doubt heavy in every glorious aspect.

Wealth and Glory

I was nonetheless surprised to find that the first place the word glory is mentioned is when somebody starts to come into abundance in the natural.

Why is there a connection with glory and wealth?

I believe it's because God is always out to *increase* both spiritual and physical wealth and weightiness among His people. It's simply one more glorious aspect of the weightiness of God, one more aspect that cannot and must not be separated from the rest of God.

But there is a purpose even for natural wealth. The reason so many Christians have misunderstood wealth stems from a lack of understanding; and this comes from witnessing the frequent misuse of wealth. Too many people end up *lusting* after material things. But does that mean that God does not have a divine purpose behind even material wealth? Absolutely not.

It's an interesting fact that in times past many Christians believed that all things pertaining to sexual intercourse between a man and a woman were evil, just because they were so often perverted and misused. But is sex really evil, or is it something ordained and blessed by God Himself?

In like manner, wealth itself is not evil when it's used to continue God's blessings to others and increase His weightiness on the earth.

Let's face it, most of the people that God used in the Old Testament were wealthy people in the natural. Everywhere they went they in turn increased **God's** weightiness and influence. Such was the case of Joseph in the house of Potiphar.

And the LORD was with Joseph, and he was a prosperous man; and he was in the house of his master the Egyptian.

And his master saw that the LORD was with him, and that the LORD made all that he did to prosper in his hand.

And Joseph found grace in his sight, and he served him: and he made him overseer over his house, and all that he had he put into his hand.

And it came to pass from the time that he had made him overseer in his house, and over all that he had, that the LORD blessed the Egyptian's house for Joseph's sake; and the blessing of the LORD was upon all that he had in the house, and in the field.

Genesis 39:2-5 (KJV)

Joseph had the same glorious blessing from Abraham that his father Jacob had. As a result of his blessing, even his Egyptian master prospered. Why? For Joseph's sake, and for the sake of the blessing from God in order to identify the one on whom God had His hand.

Regrettably, as God's people get blessed, those around them often seem to get jealous because the blessings of God are so evident upon their lives. Such was the case with Laban's sons.

And he heard the words of Laban's sons, saying, Jacob hath taken away all that was our father's; and of that which was our father's hath he gotten all this glory.

And Jacob beheld the countenance of Laban, and, behold, it was not toward him as before.

And the LORD said unto Jacob, Return unto the land of thy fathers, and to thy kindred; and I will be with thee.

Genesis 31:1-3 (KJV)

Remember, this is the first place in the Old Testament where the word glory is specifically mentioned, and it is in connection with wealth.

"He has acquired all this *glory*."

Thus it's clear that wealth can be connected with glory, and this is seen in the Bible many times.

Moses and God's Glory

As we have seen, the word glory also means *weightiness.*

Yet another definition from Strong's is copiousness, which means abundance and plentifulness. One could *hardly argue* that there was a weightiness, abundance and plentiful aspect to Jacob's increase. Furthermore, these aspects of the essence of God's glory are even more apparent in the narrative dealing with Moses and God's glory.

And Moses said to the LORD, Behold, You say to me, Bring up this people. And You have not told me whom You will send with me. Yet You have said, I know you by name, and you have also found grace in My sight.

Now therefore, I pray You, if I have found grace in Your sight, make me see now Your ways, that I may know You, that I may find grace in Your sight. And consider that this nation [is] Your people.

And He said, My presence shall go [with you], and I will give you rest.

And he said to Him, If Your presence does not go [with me], do not carry us up from here.

For in what shall it be known that I and Your people have found grace in Your sight? [Is it] not in that You go with us? So we shall be separated, I and Your people, from all the people that [are] upon the face of the earth.

And the LORD said to Moses, I will do this thing also that you have spoken. For you have found grace in My sight, and I know you by name.

And he said, I beseech You, let me see Your glory.
Exodus 33:12-18 (MKJV)

Show me your glory! But I thought God had already done just that.

Look at what Moses had seen already.

He saw a burning bush that was not consumed in the fire. Then Moses went to Egypt where God told him to throw down his rod and it turned into a serpent. When he picked it back up, it turned into a rod again. God told him to put his hand in his robe; he did and then pulled it out leprous. He put it back in again and pulled it out clean. He saw the ten mighty plagues on Egypt. He saw the Red Sea part and the water divided and congealed (froze). He saw the host of Pharaoh's armies destroyed in the water. He saw the cloud by day and the pillar of fire by night; and he received manna from heaven.

So how, after all of these incredible, miraculous signs and wonders can he ask God to show him His glory? How much of God's glory does he have to see? Remember that glory also implies weightiness, splendor, abundance and plentifulness. It was as if he was saying, "God, show me your full weightiness and splendor."

And he said to the elders, "Wait here for us until we come back to you. Indeed, Aaron and Hur are with you. If any man has a difficulty, let him go to them."

Then Moses went up into the mountain, and a cloud covered the mountain.

Now the glory of the LORD rested on Mount Sinai, and the cloud covered it six days. And on

the seventh day He called to Moses out of the midst of the cloud.

The sight of the glory of the LORD was like a consuming fire on the top of the mountain in the eyes of the children of Israel.

So Moses went into the midst of the cloud and went up into the mountain. And Moses was on the mountain forty days and forty nights.

Exodus 24:14-18

The cloud usually *covers* the glory. It is like a veil around the glory. It veils or covers what God is actually doing inside. The *cloud* could best be described as the *Presence* of God; but the glory is the manifestation of the *Person* of God.

Some cannot even see the cloud. Others see it but don't go in, yet there are some that venture in to experience God's glory: His weightiness and His splendor.

Then Moses said to the LORD, "See, You say to me, 'Bring up this people.' But You have not let me know whom You will send with me. Yet You have said, 'I know you by name, and you have also found grace in My sight.'

"Now therefore, I pray, if I have found grace in Your sight, show me now Your way, that I may know You and that I may find grace in Your sight. And consider that this nation is Your people."

And He said, "My Presence will go with you, and I will give you rest."

Then he said to Him, "If Your Presence does not go with us, do not bring us up from here.

"For how then will it be known that Your people and I have found grace in Your sight, except

You go with us? So we shall be separate, Your people and I, from all the people who are upon the face of the earth."

Exodus 33:12-16

Moses said "God I will not go anywhere without Your Presence."

Moses practically *lived* in the presence of God, and He is telling God "I won't go without you." This statement shows us just how much Moses *valued* the presence of God. Moses placed value on God's glory because he recognized all the weight, abundance and splendor that God's glory conveyed.

Remember that God spoke with Moses face to face as with a friend.

Then He said, "I will make all My goodness pass before you, and I will proclaim the name of the LORD before you. I will be gracious to whom I will be gracious, and I will have compassion on whom I will have compassion."

Exodus 33:19

Notice the word goodness. Without a doubt, goodness is also a part of God's weightiness and splendor.

But He said, "You cannot see My face; for no man shall see Me, and live."

And the LORD said, "Here is a place by Me, and you shall stand on the rock.

"So it shall be, while My glory passes by, that I will put you in the cleft of the rock, and will cover you with My hand while I pass by.

"Then I will take away My hand, and you shall see My back; but My face shall not be seen."

Exodus 33:20-23

What happens to Moses after this? Moses comes down from the mountain with a veil over his face, because the glory of God is shining from his face so brightly that no one could stand to look upon him. The people are actually seeing *his* face shine with the glory of God.

Now it was so, when Moses came down from Mount Sinai (and the two tablets of the Testimony were in Moses' hand when he came down from the mountain), that Moses did not know that the skin of his face shone while he talked with Him.

So when Aaron and all the children of Israel saw Moses, behold, the skin of his face shone, and they were afraid to come near him.

Then Moses called to them, and Aaron and all the rulers of the congregation returned to him; and Moses talked with them.

Afterward all the children of Israel came near, and he gave them as commandments all that the LORD had spoken with him on Mount Sinai.

And when Moses had finished speaking with them, he put a veil on his face.

But whenever Moses went in before the LORD to speak with Him, he would take the veil off until he came out; and he would come out and speak to the children of Israel whatever he had been commanded.

And whenever the children of Israel saw the face of Moses, that the skin of Moses' face shone, then Moses would put the veil on his face again, until he went in to speak with Him.

Exodus 34:29-35

Soon after his face is shining with the glory of God, he tells all the people who are willing to bring an offering before the Lord.

"Take from among you an offering to the LORD. Whoever is of a willing heart, let him bring it as an offering to the LORD: gold, silver, and bronze."

Exodus 35:5

Here Moses' face is shining with the glory of God and he tells the people, "I have been with God and the glory, the weightiness of God, the splendor of God, is all over me. The glory of God is beaming from me, so now I want you to bring an offering. All those with a willing heart bring an offering."

So they get excited and start bringing their offerings. They start bringing *so much* that finally Moses has to tell them to stop bringing their offerings, because they have more than enough. Their willingness to bring their treasures made a way for the glory of God to abide in the tabernacle. Remember these things had natural weightiness and splendor.

So what does this mean? People came along in the natural, bringing natural weightiness and splendor that belonged to God, and thus making provision for the return: the *pressed down, shaken together* measure that He would distribute back to them.

Then everyone came whose heart was stirred, and everyone whose spirit was willing, and they brought the LORD'S offering for the work of the tabernacle of meeting, for all its service, and for the holy garments.

They came, both men and women, as many as had a willing heart, and brought earrings and nose rings, rings and necklaces, all jewelry of gold, that

is, every man who made an offering of gold to the LORD.

Exodus 35:21,22

Then Moses called Bezalel and Aholiab, and every gifted artisan in whose heart the LORD had put wisdom, everyone whose heart was stirred, to come and do the work.

And they received from Moses all the offering which the children of Israel had brought for the work of the service of making the sanctuary. So they continued bringing to him freewill offerings every morning.

Exodus 36:2,3

and they spoke to Moses, saying, "The people bring much more than enough for the service of the work which the LORD commanded us to do."

So Moses gave a commandment, and they caused it to be proclaimed throughout the camp, saying, "Let neither man nor woman do any more work for the offering of the sanctuary." And the people were restrained from bringing,

for the material they had was sufficient for all the work to be done— indeed too much.

Exodus 36:5-7

Too much, or more than enough?

Perhaps more than anything, this reveals the essence of God's glory. God is a God who is more than enough and is willing to fill us so full that we *reflect* His glory. As we do, we begin to catch a revelation of the glory we're reflecting; we begin to understand that this was God's plan in us from the very beginning.

Chapter 2
Heavyweights

The Ultimate Heavyweight

It is difficult to imagine trying to answer the question, "How much does God weigh?"

In the sport of boxing they have what is referred to as weight divisions, or weight classes. This insures the participants that they will not be matched with an opponent that is much larger than they are. The lightest are referred to as "feather weights," but the heaviest are referred to as "heavy weights." Interestingly, the heavy weight matches are the fights that usually attract the most attention, and therefore make the most money.

In what weight class do you suppose God is? Who can challenge Him?

God is the *ultimate* heavyweight. He is omnipotent, omnipresent, omniscient and all powerful. He is Jehovah Jireh, Jehovah Nissi, Jehovah El Shaddai, Jehovah Tsidkenu, Jehovah Shammah.

He is our righteousness, our sanctifier. He is our peace. He is our joy. All of these things contribute to His glory or His weight.

One might also consider it this way: God is *heavy* with joy. God is *heavy* with faith, hope and especially love.

Likewise, according to First John 4:8, God *is* love. If God is love and He is also omnipresent, that seems to suggest that He has an *unlimited* supply of love. And an unlimited supply is very heavy.

In truth, no matter what God has or does, He is heavy with it.

He is even heavy with judgment. If you mess with Him, fire comes down from heaven and the ground opens up and swallows you. But thank God, He is even heavier with mercy. Actually, God is as heavy as His breath. Or even more precisely, God is as heavy as His Word, which is inspired or God breathed. So in this way one could say that God's breath is filled with the weightiness of His spirit.

Ever-Increasing Glory

God is looking for someone who will make way for the glory and weightiness of God to be poured out.

Notice what Jesus prays in John 17:22:

And I do not pray for these alone, but for those also who shall believe on Me through their word,

that they all may be one, as You, Father, [are] in Me, and I in You, that they also may be one in Us, so that the world may believe that You have sent Me.

And I have given them the glory which You have given Me, that they may be one, even as We are one,

I in them, and You in Me, that they may be made perfect in one; and that the world may know that You have sent Me and have loved them as You have loved Me.

John 17:20-23 (MKJV)

Jesus said the *glory* that you gave to Me, I gave to them. He's saying, "All that I have and all that I am in full weight, honor, splendor, abundance and plentiful-ness, I gave to you!"

Up until now, we have focused more on the Old Testament manifestation of God's glory in cases like Abraham and Moses. However, I believe there's a greater dimension of God's glory coming in the New Covenant than there ever was with Moses.

God is ever-expanding, ever-growing and ever-increasing.

Why should we experience less than what was available to Moses?

By the time we get into the New Covenant, the glory of God is more intense and on a greater dimension. God is continually expanding up and out. God is continually increasing. God does not stop expanding.

For example, in the beginning when God said, "Let there be light," the way in which He said this implies a continuous presence of light. It essentially means light *was* from that moment on. Hebrew words can sometimes be used in a way that means a continuous existence of the thing mentioned. So if God said "Let there be light," there was light, and God has never taken His words back.

God's Word will not return void. If God's Word goes to a place that is void, where there is nothing, it isn't going to return void. It is going to fill the darkness; it is going to fill the void. Wherever God's Word goes, it will fill that void, creating a new reality. Keep in mind that the Word that fills this void was propelled by His breath.

That means that He is ever-expanding similar to light which is still travelling at three hundred and eighty six thousand miles per second or three times ten to the eight meters per second.

God is ever-increasing in splendor, in abundance and in blessing. He's getting weightier and weightier all of the time. His weight is still growing, it's not stopping. If God is ever-increasing, then so is the glory that He has given us.

And we, who with unveiled faces all reflect the Lord's glory, are being transformed into His likeness with ever-increasing glory, which comes from the Lord, who is the Spirit.
2 Corinthians 3:18 (NIV)

So what does God see when he looks at us? God looks at us as little gods: He sees a *reflection* of Himself. He looks at us and sees the potential of Himself within us. God looks at us as children being transformed into His likeness. We share His glory, therefore, we share in His unlimited potential.

as His divine power has given to us all things that pertain to life and godliness, through the knowledge of Him who called us by glory and virtue. **2 Peter 1:3**

But His boundaries and His weight are always going to exceed ours. He is always going to be the Father, because He went before us. So our splendor and glory will follow after His and originate from His Spirit.

If our Father is a heavyweight, then that is exactly what His children must grow up to be: heavyweights.

Mysteries

However, we speak wisdom among those who are mature, yet not the wisdom of this age, nor of the rulers of this age, who are coming to nothing.

But we speak the wisdom of God in a mystery, the hidden wisdom which God ordained before the ages for our glory,

18

which none of the rulers of this age knew; for had they known, they would not have crucified the Lord of glory.

1 Corinthians 2:6-8

Who did God ordain the wisdom of the ages for? Who did God ordain the mysteries and the answers to the mysteries for? It was the hidden wisdom, which God ordained for *our* glory. Why would it be for our glory?

Howbeit we speak the wisdom among them that are perfect: yet not the wisdom of this world, nor the princes of this world, that come to nought:

But we speak the wisdom of God in a *mystery*, even the hidden wisdom, which God ordained before the world unto our glory:

1 Corinthians 2:6,7(KJV)

it is God's wisdom that I speak therefore the secret is made known to the people.

Verse 6 (Con)

We speak the wisdom that came from God once a covered secret, but now is uncovered ,

Verse 7 (Wms)

The word mysteries in Greek is *musterion*. According to Strong's, it comes from a derivative of muo (to shut the mouth); and means a secret or "mystery" (through the idea of silence imposed by initiation into religious rites).

There were secret fraternal organizations before the time of Jesus in Greek communities, much like what we have today in the Masons. These clubs had secrets, and in order to know the secrets you had to have the code. They took this word "musterion" from this setting.

But the Bible says that it has been given unto us to know the musterion.

That means that we have the code from God through the Holy Spirit to unlock all mysteries.

"Therefore do not fear them. For there is nothing covered that will not be revealed, and hidden that will not be known."

Matthew 10:26

But we speak the wisdom of God in a mystery, the hidden wisdom which God ordained before the ages for our glory,

which none of the rulers of this age knew; for had they known, they would not have crucified the Lord of glory.

But as it is written: "Eye has not seen, nor ear heard, nor have entered into the heart of man the things which God has prepared for those who love Him."

1 Corinthians 2:7-9

Those who love Him abide in His love; they come into the secret place and those mysteries can be unlocked.

But God has revealed them to us through His Spirit. For the Spirit searches all things, yes, the deep things of God.

For what man knows the things of a man except the spirit of the man which is in him? Even so no one knows the things of God except the Spirit of God.

Now we have received, not the spirit of the world, but the Spirit who is from God, that we might know the things that have been freely given to us by God.

1 Corinthians 2:10-12

Why did He say that we might know all the things that have been freely given to us by God?

Because He *wants* us to know all the things that have been freely given to us by God.

It is not like He is saying, "I don't want you to know." He is saying, "I want you to know." It isn't a mystery any longer, because He is saying, "I want you to know it." God is not out to hide things.

Unveiling the Glory

The devil is the one trying to hide things from us. One of the things he does is to set up false visions and distractions to keep us from understanding that these mysteries and this wisdom of God are ordained for our glory. The devil doesn't want us to reflect the splendor and the weightiness of God, which is for our glory.

His job is to put a veil up to prevent us from reflecting God's glory.

The devil doesn't want glory to be unlocked and exposed. He doesn't want that glory to be manifested and revealed to us, or through us. He'll do whatever he can, however he can, to cover it up.

Moses wore a veil over his face and the Bible says that the glory upon Moses would fade away because it was only temporal. But the glory we are speaking of now is stronger.

And we, who with *unveiled faces* all reflect the Lord's glory, are being transformed into His likeness with ever-increasing glory, which comes from the Lord, who is the Spirit.

2 Corinthians 3:18 (NIV)

In The New Testament, the word glory is generally translated from the Greek word *doxa*. Doxa is used to translate the Hebrew Kabowd. In the above verse it implies the divine beaming and shining forth of the rays of God's divine nature. God wants His full weight to *shine forth* through us.

The devil knows that we are still in the flesh, so he will come along and try to convince us that we are still sinners. I'm saved by grace, which is the divine influence upon my heart and its reflection in my life. Under grace I won't see myself as I was, but I will see myself as God sees me. Grace will change your way of thinking.

The devil is also going to have us meditate and look upon other people's sin. The first thing that he tries to do is get us into competitive jealousy. He has to get us to start comparing ourselves with each other.

His whole strategy is to slowly work his vision of the power of death within us. The devil has lied to the body...that's his job.

If we had the chance to see someone who was nine hundred years old, then we would suddenly believe that we could live until we were nine hundred years old. Our belief system would no longer prevent us from seeing the opportunity for life. Long life would be unveiled.

God is speaking, and His words are unveiling the glory. God is unlocking and revealing secrets. God intends for us to live forever. God intends for this glorious body to destroy death beneath its feet. We are the fullness of the All in All; and all things have been put beneath His feet. As He says, "That we might know the love of Christ and be filled with all the fullness of God" (Ephesians 3:19).

If we are filled with God's fullness, then we share in His heaviness and glory. Like Him, we also are now heavyweights.

Chapter 3
The Glory Paradigm

A paradigm, in the strictest sense of the word, is a model or example of something that functions as a pattern. I believe that God's glory is essentially a paradigm or pattern for understanding more about God.

Let's take another look at material wealth. It has often been said that man wouldn't have had any idea to place more value on gold and diamonds than ordinary rocks if it hadn't been for God revealing something about the rarity and splendor of certain stones and metals to him. Gold and diamonds are valuable because they are both rare and beautiful. Likewise, God is full of qualities that are both rare and beautiful compared to ordinary man.

His glory is evidence of this. In this manner, it serves to help us understand that God is not lacking in any good thing. When we begin to get a revelation of the glory paradigm, we can begin to act in light of that same abundant and plentiful example.

The Power and the Glory

In the New Testament, when the Church had revival that continued from the Day of Pentecost, something very similar happened to the disciples that happened to the Israelites under Moses: the people brought all that they

23

possessed and laid it at the disciple's feet. Why did that happen?

The disciples were walking in grace with demonstrations of great power. This was not a dead religious social gathering. The Church was living in power.

And they continued steadfastly in the apostles' doctrine and fellowship, in the breaking of bread, and in prayers.

Then fear came upon every soul, and many wonders and signs were done through the apostles.

Acts 2:42,43

In Acts 4:29, the apostles were praying that they would be granted boldness to speak the Word and that signs and wonders would come through their hands.

This discourse continues on to say that believers were added. The Bible says signs and wonders *follow believers*. Believers cast out devils, heal the sick and raise the dead. They emanate power and live in great grace.

It's one thing to say that you're a believer and another thing to walk in the power and grace of a believer. Obviously the Church in the book of Acts was not playing games. What was so different?

There was unity and they understood covenant.

They had all things in common and salvation's root was one of power.

The apostles were living with Christ by the power of God demonstrated to all. (Take Peter for instance; as he walked down the street he emanated the power and glory of God.)

Now the multitude of those who believed were of one heart and one soul; neither did anyone say

24

that any of the things he possessed was his own, but they had all things in common.

And with great power the apostles gave witness to the resurrection of the Lord Jesus. And great grace was upon them all.

Nor was there anyone among them who lacked; for all who were possessors of lands or houses sold them, and brought the proceeds of the things that were sold,

and laid them at the apostles' feet; and they distributed to each as anyone had need.

Acts 4:32-35

Rather than storing up wealth in fear, God's people caught a revelation of the abundance of God. Consequently, they sold their goods and gave to others who had a need. They began to understand that there was no reason for any of them to lack. God had already placed enough wealth within the group. As soon as they acted as one group or one body, everyone had more than enough. In God there is no lack, *and His body should be a reflection of Him.*

Again we see a unique connection between God's glory and material goods. However, do not misunderstand me. I am *not* implying that everyone with material wealth is godly, or that all material wealth was righteously obtained therefore attracting God's glory. The lust for material wealth can certainly destroy one's soul. I'm talking about the natural results of seeking God with a right motive, reflecting His glory and walking in covenant.

When we seek God, He adds his weight. In this way, the glory paradigm is reflected in us.

But seek first the kingdom of God and His righteousness, and all these things shall be added to you.

Matthew 6:33

God is truly all about increase; therefore, you cannot always separate wealth from glory. Just as the above verse confirms, seek God first and "things" will be added to you. As in the natural, so in the spirit.

The tangible things necessary *to increase* God's kingdom, the wealth and splendor, are just natural manifestations of God, because God is unlimited. God is not about to let those who are increasing His kingdom lack the natural glory they need to fulfill His task. Wherever He guides, His glory provides.

Power in Glory

The children of Israel gave willingly of their goods to prepare the tabernacle of God. After Moses gathered the offering, he built the Ark of the Covenant.

Once the Tabernacle was built and the ark was there, the glory filled the Tabernacle.

And he raised up the court all around the tabernacle and the altar, and hung up the screen of the court gate. So Moses finished the work.

Then the cloud covered the tabernacle of meeting, and the glory of the LORD filled the tabernacle.

And Moses was not able to enter the tabernacle of meeting, because the cloud rested above it, and the glory of the LORD filled the tabernacle.

Exodus 40:33-35

The glory or splendor of the Lord, the Kabowd, filled the tabernacle. But as we have seen, glory is much more than that. The wealth, weightiness, plentifulness and the abundance of God filled the tabernacle.

The tabernacle was no longer a simple man-made construction divorced of any real spiritual significance. The power of God had arrived.

Much later, when Solomon completed the temple, it's recorded in Chronicles that the priests were unable to stand and perform their duties because of God's glory.

So that the priests could not stand to minister by reason of the cloud: for the glory of the LORD had filled the house of God.

2 Chronicles 5:14 (KJV)

What happened to cause the glory of the Lord to fill the house so completely that the priests could not even carry out their duties?

God's weightiness was increased. Notice what happened in the verse prior to this:

and [they] were as one to the trumpeters and to the singers, to make one sound to be heard in praising and thanking the LORD; and as they lifted up [their] voice with the trumpets and cymbals and instruments of music, and praised the LORD, [saying], For He is good, for His mercy [endures] forever, the house was filled with a cloud, the house of the LORD.

2 Chronicles 5:13

The people spared no expense in building God's temple; and afterwards they sowed their praises in unity.

It's very important to remember that natural weight from a willing heart built the Ark of the Covenant, so that the spiritual weight (God's presence and glory), would have a place to abide.

27

Likewise, as we are willing to bring natural weight to God's kingdom, more space will be made available for the spiritual weight. This, of course, is in no way an attempt to buy God's glory. It is, in essence, a supernatural result from an act of worship.

Notice what the Apostle Paul writes in Romans concerning us, the vessels of His mercy:

What if he [God] did this to make the riches of his glory known to the objects of his mercy, whom he prepared in advance for glory.

Romans 9:23 (NIV)

We are the vessels of His mercy that have been prepared for glory in advance!

Why is God preparing us for glory or weightiness?

The time has arrived for Him to turn up His power and anointing on the earth. And if the power is about to be increased, the "vessels" that hold this power must be prepared.

We must in essence, be prepared to reflect a divine glory that is weighty in all of its numerous aspects, in wealth, heaviness, splendor and abundance.

When spiritual weight comes into place, natural weight comes to us for us to take dominion.

Arise, shine; for your light has come! And the glory of the LORD is risen upon you.

For behold, the darkness shall cover the earth, and deep darkness the people; but the LORD will arise over you, and His glory will be seen upon you.

The Gentiles shall come to your light, and kings to the brightness of your rising.

"Lift up your eyes all around, and see: they all gather together, they come to you; your sons shall come from afar, and your daughters shall be nursed at your side.

"Then you shall see and become radiant, and your heart shall swell with joy; because the abundance of the sea shall be turned to you, the wealth of the Gentiles shall come to you.

"The multitude of camels shall cover your land, the dromedaries of Midian and Ephah; all those from Sheba shall come; they shall bring gold and incense, and they shall proclaim the praises of the LORD.

"All the flocks of Kedar shall be gathered together to you, the rams of Nebaioth shall minister to you; they shall ascend with acceptance on My altar, and I will glorify the house of My glory.

"Who are these who fly like a cloud, and like doves to their roosts?

"Surely the coastlands shall wait for Me; and the ships of Tarshish will come first, to bring your sons from afar, their silver and their gold with them, to the name of the LORD your God, and to the Holy One of Israel, because He has glorified you."

Isaiah 60:1-9

Chapter 4
Increasing God's Weightiness

Yielding to God's Weightiness

What happens when you increase God's kingdom? What happens when you increase God's weightiness on earth?

You are bringing God weight, which means that you will have to make weighty decisions. But in order to do this, you will have to yield to God's weightiness.

To yield means to give way to some other power. But what does yielding to God's weightiness involve? I believe it involves both knowing the love of Christ and being filled with the fullness of God. It only makes sense that the more we know about Christ's love and the more we are filled with God's fullness, the easier it will be to give way to God's glory that is already present within us. If we know the love of Christ; and we're filled with all the fullness of God, then how in the world are we going to die?

I don't believe that God was trying to hold it back from us, because in Ephesians it says, "That we might know the love of Christ, that we might be filled with all the fullness of God."

If God wants to put everything beneath our feet, then He is going to put death beneath our feet as well.

Death is the sting of sin. It's a barrier that is being broken. Remember, the weightiness of God is stronger than death. I don't believe that we have a full concept of how weighty God is, how big God wants to get in us and how many barriers He wants to defy.

People today are tied so tightly to the world. The devil uses things like drugs and medicine every way he can to get people bound. Some people can't live without a pill a day and the devil has found a way to bind them to that.

People forget who sickness belongs to. We need to yield to the weight of God. We need to yield to healing. It should never be easier to yield to the doctor rather than God.

Changing Our Perception

In order for us to yield to the weightiness of God, we must change our perception. What am I trying to say? In order to give way to God, we must *see* things differently. This is because we are a visual generation.

A lot of people today are like Thomas. "Let me see the holes in your feet. Let me see somebody go flying through the air. Let me see that this is for real and then I will believe." Then when they do see that it's real, they only believe for about a day or two until something comes along to sway them the other way. What happened? They slid back to their finite perception.

The devil has them meditate on someone who is messed up and crippled. He has them meditate on the power of something that's dysfunctional. They might have seen a miracle a month ago at church, but over the course of the month, the devil had them meditate upon everyone else who was sick and every form of *his* power. When you get ready to pray for them, they've forgotten about the miracle and the devil has stripped their faith bare. They meditate upon and perceive the powers of the enemy.

That's the whole idea behind the secular news broadcast. It's continually reminding you of tornadoes, murder, etc. They have to show you man's flaws and dysfunction, so they set up entire broadcasts to show you just how bad, bad can be.

But God wants to unlock mysteries for our glory. The devil is working, unlocking the power of the flesh. God wants to unveil the Spirit and the glory and weightiness of that Spirit.

He wants to change our perception. He wants us to see the power of that anointing and the seeds that He has placed inside of us.

That's why, when Paul came to that town in Acts 17, he said, "I perceive that you have faith to be healed; get up and walk," and the man got up and walked. When the man started walking, the people in the town began to bring their animals to sacrifice because they thought that the gods had come down from heaven.

But all along, something is happening. They're beginning to see God. Paul is not getting caught up with them beginning to see things in the flesh. He even tears his clothes and says, "We are men like you are. It's God doing this through us."

God wants to be glorified through the flesh, not the flesh be glorified in flesh. The devil will glorify and magnify the flesh. The secular news is very good in assisting him.

Our Light Has Come

God is trying to do something big inside of us, but we can't get caught up with what is binding us in the natural. The Bible says that if we love the world, then the love of the Father is not in us.

Sometimes we love the things of the world, and that is the whole intention of the devil. That might even mean loving other people's fleshly, material things.

We have become a very morbid society because we thrive on dysfunction. If something is a mess we go to it. Let's get the news on it!

We have not understood the power of those things; and God is trying to do something big and miraculous inside of us. We need to get that really clear.

If you allow seeds of death to be sown into you, you will reap death. If you allow seeds of life to be sown into you, you will reap life.

Sowing weightiness, splendor and abundance has made the way for Isaiah 60:1-3:

Arise, shine; for your light has come! And the glory of the LORD is risen upon you. [This is what will be the result when we reap glory.]

For behold, the darkness shall cover the earth, and deep darkness the people; but the LORD will arise over you, and His glory will be seen upon you.

The Gentiles shall come to your light, and kings to the brightness of your rising.

Isaiah 60:1-3

"The Gentiles shall come to your light." This is the result of partaking of grace, which was previously defined from *Strong's Concordance* as the divine influence upon the heart and its reflection in the life. You received when you sowed glory.

I am wondering why the Gentiles, or those without God, aren't coming?

God is trying to reveal His glory, His splendor and His weightiness. He's trying to reveal all that He is.

He's trying to reveal His abundance and His plentifulness. Why do you think God said that the wealth of the
wicked is laid up for the just?

The Muslims and Hindus have a thing in the United
States right now where they're trying to buy up all the
property that they can. They believe that property rep-
resents their god. Therefore the more property they
own, the more there is that belongs to their god.

This is simply a perversion of what God promises.
God told Joshua to go into all the world and take dominion. He told them that everywhere their feet trod
belonged to them. God is into land too. God is into
property. I believe that God wants this whole earth to be
in the hands of those who are righteous. If we control
the property, we'll control the dominion of the earth. No
wickedness will be able to mess with our property. God
has a plan for all land to belong to those in Christ.

Because Jacob was being blessed, they called that
glory. God wants to pour out His weightiness on His
people. When the weightiness of God comes on you, it
isn't just going to come on you in healing and deliver-
ance or salvation, it's going to come on you in wealth.
When the glory of God comes all over you, the wealth of
God is going to come all over you. Money will come to
you like you can't believe, as long as you just do what
God tells you to do and seek Him first in everything.

The Latter Glory

**"Lift up your eyes all around, and see: they all
gather together, they come to you; your sons shall
come from afar, and your daughters shall be
nursed at your side.**

**"Then you shall see and become radiant, and
your heart shall swell with joy; because the abun-**

dance of the sea shall be turned to you, the wealth of the Gentiles shall come to you."

Isaiah 60:4,5

This is all connected with glory. You cannot separate wealth from glory. This is the kind of God we have. "I will bless those who bless you, and I will curse those who curse you."

He is out to eliminate and remove the veils of corruption. He is out to bring clarity.

What makes God so weighty? How heavy does God weigh?

The Holy Spirit told me He is as big as His ability to create. Whatever He can create and continue to create, that's how heavy He is. He's as heavy as all that He can create. That's how heavy He is, and He doesn't stop there.

Just like I said before, He is ever-expanding, ever-increasing and He is ever continually getting heavier. I believe the weight of God that was experienced in the Old Testament is nothing compared to the weight of God that God wants revealed in His children and through His children, before Jesus returns.

"'The glory of this latter temple shall be greater than the former,' says the LORD of hosts. 'And in this place I will give peace,' says the LORD of hosts."

Haggai 2:9

This is not just talking about greater, it is talking about ever-increasing. This is why the devil is trying to rob vision.

This is why the devil wants people to get caught up with the dysfunction of the flesh. He is trying to glorify whatever sin can attach itself to. Whatever powers that sin can move in — that is what the devil is trying to glorify. He's continually trying to glorify the power of sin. He would have us meditate on every power of sin that he has.

That's his whole idea, to set before us the power of sin and the works of sin and what sin has accomplished and is doing through man and through all his works. But remember God's word through the Prophet Haggai:

"The future glory of this Temple will be greater than its past glory, says the LORD Almighty. And in this place I will bring peace. I, the LORD Almighty, have spoken!"

Haggai 2:9 (NLT)

and in this place I will give peace — it is Yahweh Sabaoth who speaks.

(TJB)

The latter glory of this house [with its success, to which Jesus came] shall be greater than the former....

(AMP)

in this place will I grant prosperity, this is the very Word of the Lord of Hosts.

(NEB)

This word glory is *kabowd*. This is talking about the weightiness of God, the splendor of God; the abundance and the splendor of God is going to be *greater* in the latter house. The reason that the glory is greater is because we are no longer under the Old Covenant favor. We are now under New Covenant grace. In the Old Covenant, it was God's favor, but in the New Covenant, we have a right to come into the throne room to receive divine influence upon our heart and its reflection in our life.

However, before we can receive greater glory, God requires that we give a seed of glory.

"The silver is Mine, and the gold is Mine," says the LORD of hosts.

Haggai 2:8

"All gold and silver are Mine." It all belongs to God. People say "we want the glory," but God is saying, "It's all Mine. It all needs to come to My feet. It all needs to come to Me. It all needs to belong to the righteous. It all needs to belong to the children of God." That's the same idea perverted by the Muslims and the Hindus. As far as they're concerned, if Allah gets more land, that shows that he has more power. That shows that their god is bigger and bigger.

"And you shall remember the LORD your God, for it is He who gives you power to get wealth, that He may establish His covenant which He swore to your fathers, as it is this day."

Deuteronomy 8:18

Always remember that it is the LORD your God who gives you power to become rich, and he does it to fulfill the covenant he made with your ancestors.

Deuteronomy 8:18 (NLT)

We have this treasure in earthen vessels that the excellency of power may be of God and not of man. So God has given us His ability to be weighty.

Why is He going to unlock mysteries? For our glory. He's going to unlock all the secrets because we're part of the mystery. That means that He has given us the key, by the Spirit of God, to unlock all mysteries for our glory. What does it mean *for our glory*? God wants to be weighty in us. That's why He said, "Arise and shine, for thy light is come." He wants His glory and His weight to be *in us*.

Giving Minded

For us to experience the fullness of the latter glory, we must have a mindset *like* God's.

First we have to be blessing minded *inside* before we can be blessing minded *outside*. We have to have His abundant mentality inside of us before we can have abundance outside.

We have to think like a billionaire giver on the inside, before we can experience anything on the outside. We first have to have a *giving* mentality inside. We have to yield to the Spirit of God, the same Spirit that says, "For God so loved the world that He gave." That Spirit of giving has to come inside and explode.

I asked God, "How do I give you glory?" The first thing that He told me was that when you sow seed, you are not just sowing seed, but you are sowing glory and you are bringing God an offering of weightiness. That is why all those with a *willing heart* received the glory in the Ark of the Covenant. What happened when they willingly brought an offering? The glory of God showed up in the Tabernacle.

"God, I give you this seed. I give you weightiness. I give you splendor. I give you abundance. I give you plentifulness. Here is my seed, for you know the potential in that seed."

God knows how much weight that seed can carry. He knows how much ability is in that seed. He knows how many people that seed can touch. He also knows the value of that seed and the sacrifice behind that seed. We need to start thinking like Him.

When we sow seed, we increase weightiness on another person's life. What did Laban's sons say about

Jacob?" Look at all this glory that Jacob has obtained. Look at all this kabowd that Jacob has obtained, all this weightiness." What did Jacob obtain? His flocks just kept growing. His lambs kept growing and increasing and they called that glory. He started getting weighty with wealth. This is the Old Testament. We aren't even dealing with the latter glory yet. If God gets weighty in us, He's going to get weighty all around us. If God gets weighty in us, the blessings of God will get heavy all around us.

When you sow seed, you give that person the ability to do what God has called them to do. That means that you give them weight. When you give, it shall be given unto you. What's that about? When you give God glory, then God desires to pour out some glory and some weightiness on you. He desires to pour out His splendor and abundance and plentifulness on you, because when you give, you give Him glory. He then pours out His blessings on you, pressed down, shaken together and running over.

Does God necessarily always give you money back? No, sometimes He gives you another form of weightiness back. For instance, He might give divine influence of His ideas. But it's from the same essence of His glory, always in plentifulness and abundance.

Sowing Glory

Set yourself to be giving minded by having the right mindset and attitude, always being ready to sow.

Remember the paradigm or model of sowing and reaping? This law is also in one sense a reflection of God. The law of sowing is a means for providing abundance, weightiness and increase. For instance, when you sow with a perpetual giving spirit, expect to receive a perpetual harvest and you *will reap* what was sown. Think about this for a moment.

When you sow seed you are in essence sowing glory, so you will reap glory. Did you catch that? When you sow finances you are sowing one kind of kabowd. You are sowing natural weightiness, abundance and plentifulness into another person's life.

However, when you reap you will reap *both* natural and supernatural weightiness, splendor and glory.

Most people don't understand giving; they think that it's somebody trying to get their money. In actuality, no one is trying to get your money — they're trying to get you free to *receive glory pressed down, shaken together and running over.*

Remember that the weightiness you are sowing will help them to accomplish the vision and bear fruit.

(There is an anointing that's pulsating through this revelation of glory that is breaking off all dependence upon self.)

Fruit that remains brings perpetual harvest. Sow and you'll reap the results which is the fruit of what 's been sown into another person's life.

A good example of this is when a minister goes to a foreign country. Before he goes, he collects offerings for his mission trip. While he's in that foreign country, everything that happens (salvation, healing, spreading the Gospel), is the result or the fruit of the offerings that he received before leaving his home.

In this manner, *everyone* that gave into the mission trip reaps the results of what happened during the mission trip. They became *a partaker of the grace* that is upon that minister's life.

Sound unusual? Actually the concept is very old. Paul talks about this in Philippians. In chapter one verse seven he writes the following:

Just as it is right for me to think this of you all, because I have you in my heart, inasmuch as both in my chains and in the defense and confirmation of the gospel, you all are partakers with me of grace.

Philippians 1:7

In this verse, the Greek word for *grace* as defined in *Strong's Concordance* is *Charis*, which means the divine influence upon the heart and its reflection in the life.

Why were the Philippians partakers (taking a part of) and sharers of the divine favor and influence on Paul's heart? The answer lies in the last chapter of the book:

Yet it was kind of you to share my trouble.

And you Philippians yourselves know that in the beginning of the gospel, when I left Macedonia, no church entered into partnership with me in giving and receiving except you only;

for even in Thessalonica you sent me help once and again.

Philippians 4:14-16 (RSV)

The Philippians shared in Paul's trouble. How? By sending an offering. They were sowing natural glory. They were sowing seeds into Paul's ministry when no other church was supporting him. As a result of their generous giving, they shared in that same divine influence that was upon Paul's life.

Imagine for a moment having an opportunity to sow a seed into a ministry such as Paul's. It's hard to conceive that surrendering a little material wealth could help facilitate the writing of Epistles that would later touch millions of people and spark countless revivals throughout history. Imagine the harvest of God's grace that was made available to this church.

As a result of their sowing, they reaped. They were the only church to whom Paul could say this:

Not that I seek the gift; but I seek *the fruit which increases to your credit.*

I have received full payment, and more; I am filled, having received from Epaphroditus the *gifts you sent,* a fragrant offering, a sacrifice acceptable and pleasing to God.

And *my God will supply every need of yours according to his riches in glory* in Christ Jesus.

To our God and Father be glory for ever and ever. Amen.

Philippians 4:17-20 (RSV)

My God will supply all your needs according to what? *His riches in glory in Christ Jesus.* Their needs would be supplied or reaped *in glory* in Christ Jesus.

In other words, if you sow natural glory into my ministry you will reap an everlasting harvest in souls. And not only that, my God will supply your every need according to His riches in glory, in Christ Jesus!

What are God's riches in glory in Christ Jesus? God is rich *in abundance, in heaviness and in plentifulness.* And these Phillipians were the ones who were partakers of the grace of God that was on Paul's life.

I think we must be careful not to overlook how significant this statement is. One of the reasons it is so significant has to do with the importance of grace. It helps greatly to understand the importance of grace by looking at it from God's perspective. Notice what Paul says about grace in this verse from Romans:

That is why it depends on faith, in order that the promise may rest on grace and be guaranteed to all his descendants...

Romans 4:16 (RSV)

The reason salvation is by faith is because God's desire was, and always will be, to show His grace to all. Grace is even the reason for faith. Paul knew what grace would produce. It had the ability to draw God's glory. God's splendor, God's weightiness, His abundance, and His plentifulness would no doubt begin to emanate from them.

Therefore, when you sow into an anointed ministry, you can expect that same divine influence and favor on your life that is in the life of the minister to whom you are sowing. That same grace will emanate from you.

"The Gentiles shall come to your light and kings to the brightness of your rising," (Isaiah 60:3). This is a result of grace, the divine influence upon the heart and its reflection upon the life. Remember you received this because you sowed glory It will shine forth in glory, *because you gave to God.*

You will have favor all over you and favor coming out of you, because you are giving to God. When you give to God, you make room for your gift. Favor is poured out on you. The glory or weightiness of God begins to move around you. When the weightiness of God begins to move all around you, we call that favor.

Your confession should be, "I am getting heavy in God. God is getting heavy in me. I feel a heavy God. I feel a big God just getting bigger in me all of the time."

When God gets bigger in you, there is a weightiness that begins to go around you and favor begins to emanate from you so that in everything you do, people want to be a blessing to you.

For behold, the darkness shall cover the earth, and deep darkness the people; but the LORD will arise over you, and His glory will be seen upon you.

The Gentiles shall come to your light, and kings to the brightness of your rising.
Isaiah 60:2,3

They see the divine influence of grace upon the heart which reflects rays and beams of His divine glory. As this happens it draws blessings and abundance to you.

As God displays His abundance and plentifulness, He is going to give to you pressed down, shaken together and running over. In doing so, He manifests His glory!

What if you sow glory? Then you will reap glory. How do you sow glory? One of the first ways to sow glory is by sowing a seed. In this way, you are increasing the ability in another person's life for them to be able to do what God has called them to do. Through this grace, God's weight will become bigger all over the earth.

When you make a way for God's weight to get bigger all over the earth, then God is going to pour out a blessing on you pressed down, shaken together and running over. The blessing is just going to start pouring out to you. When you walk out that weightiness, that favor of God is going to be all around you. It is going to start drawing the blessings of God.

If we sow weightiness, abundance, plentifulness and splendor, then we'll reap weightiness, abundance, plentifulness and splendor.

"For as the rain comes down, and the snow from heaven, and do not return there, but water the earth, and make it bring forth and bud, that it may give seed to the sower and bread to the eater,

"So shall My word be that goes forth from My mouth; it shall not return to Me void, but it shall accomplish what I please, and it shall prosper in the thing for which I sent it."
Isaiah 55:10,11

45

He gives seed to the sower. Why? Because He's trying to bring weight to us.

"Give, and it will be given to you: good measure, pressed down, shaken together, and running over will be put into your bosom. For with the same measure that you use, it will be measured back to you."

Luke 6:38

This is why the devil fights giving tooth and nail, with everything he has. He knows that it is intricately connected with wealth and glory.

Ananias and Sapphira

Isaiah 60 verse 1 says, "Arise, shine; for your light has come! And the glory of the LORD is risen upon you." This is a result of reaping glory. This is what happened in Peter's life. Look what happened when he confronted Ananias and Sapphira when they withheld and kept for themselves the glory that belonged to God. They fell down dead at his words.

Ananias and Sapphira did not fully desire to partake of the grace, the divine influence upon the heart and its reflection in the life coming from Peter and being reflected towards them. This reflection is called Doxa in the Greek translation. I believe that in this case, it points to the glory emanating from the grace that is reflecting upon the heart and the life. Because of their selfish motives, they lied to the Holy Spirit and withheld glory when glory was being extended to them.

It's regrettable that some people's actions are the same today. Some actually believe that they can mock and make light of God's glory; thereby putting God's Spirit to the test. But if the same power and grace that was emanating in the book of Acts from the Church is present today, then we should see similar judgments when men try to use man's methods and ways.

Imagine trying to *deceive* a ministry like that of the apostles in Acts by holding back material wealth. It is very hard to imagine that Ananias and Sapphira (Acts 5) actually withheld seeds of glory from Peter and lied about the amount they received. The apostle's ministry was both powerful and foundational to everything the Church would be. Imagine the reward of glory that would have been available to Ananias and Sapphira if they had not lied.

And Joses, who was also named Barnabas by the apostles (which is translated Son of Encouragement), a Levite of the country of Cyprus,

having land, sold it, and brought the money and laid it at the apostles' feet. Acts 4:36,37

Joses was laying it at the apostle's feet to do the work of God. That is not the motive that Ananias and Sapphira had when laying their money at the apostle's feet. He was bringing weightiness, splendor, abundance and plentifulness to do the work of God. Ananias and Sapphira saw Joses do this and believed that if they did the same thing, they would receive the same status that he did. So they decided to sell their land and also lay it at the apostles' feet.

You have to understand that Peter was under a massive divine influence. He was so hooked up to heaven that the very beams and light rays of heaven were shining upon him and everywhere he walked, he experienced the reflection of it in his life. That is grace, literally, figuratively, translatory; the divine influence upon the heart and its reflection in the life. So as he walked, he cast shadows and everyone his shadow fell upon was healed. The reason that he cast shadows is because of grace. There was great grace, which brought power into his life. With great power the apostles gave witness of the resurrection of the Lord Jesus Christ and great grace was upon them. Where there is great power there is great grace.

But a certain man named Ananias, with Sapphira his wife, sold a possession.

And he kept back part of the proceeds, his wife also being aware of it, and brought a certain part and laid it at the apostles' feet.

But Peter said, "Ananias, why has Satan filled your heart to lie to the Holy Spirit and keep back part of the price of the land for yourself?

"While it remained, was it not your own? And after it was sold, was it not in your own control? Why have you conceived this thing in your heart? You have not lied to men but to God."

Then Ananias, hearing these words, fell down and breathed his last. So great fear came upon all those who heard these things.

Acts 5:1-5

When Ananias came to Peter and laid the money at his feet he did not say a word; all he did was lay it at his feet. Peter said to him, "Ananias, why has Satan filled your heart to lie to the Holy Spirit?" Peter had a word of knowledge. Ananias didn't turn and say, "I lied to you Holy Spirit, I am going to rip you off." In his heart he felt the unction to bring all he had. He was doing a good thing. He had a willing heart didn't he? Wasn't he bringing weightiness, abundance and splendor, just like the children of Israel? Those who had a willing heart brought weightiness, abundance and splendor and the glory, the *kabowd* of God came in. Immediately upon saying this to Ananias, he fell down and breathed his last breath. When his wife came in the same thing happened to her.

What gives Peter the right to tell them that this day is the last breath that they will breathe? Grace. Ananias was withholding glory. He was withholding weightiness, abundance, plentifulness and splendor from the man of God who was not withholding the anointing that produces glory. At that point he was casting shadows and healing everyone on whom his shadow fell. I believe what Ananias was saying was, "I am not going to support that ministry. I am going to hold back my money. I do not want the power of God to go into another street to release that anointing to cast shadows over other people so that they too will be healed." If you withhold the weightiness and the ability for God to take another man and put him in another street to cast another shadow to heal all the sick, God is going to do something. He has control of all the weightiness. The Bible says that He weighs the spirits in the balance. He gave you the ability and the power to create wealth, to fulfill His covenant.

That day Ananias thought, "I will take that power to create wealth and do with it what I want." When he did that, God said, "You are withholding weightiness from Me, Ananias. You are withholding abundance and splendor from Me Ananias, so I am going to withhold My weightiness, abundance and splendor from you," and immediately the breath of God left them and they fell down dead, because they thought that what they had belonged to them. Mark my words, there's coming a day in the Church when the man of God will stand behind the pulpit and say, "You liar; you withheld when power was flowing," and someone will drop down dead. Fear will fall upon the people and they will say, "We better open up our wallets," because when Ananias and Sapphira fell down dead, great fear fell upon the people. If you realize how powerful seed is and how it enables a person to do what God has called them to do, you won't hold back at all. You'll do all that you can to be a blessing. The reason that people don't fall down dead today is because great grace has not yet had its full expression through us as yet. When you see someone like Peter, then you need to find a way to make sure that they are going somewhere.

A wonderful opportunity presented itself for Ananias and Sapphira to sow glory. Instead, they sowed deceit; and as a result, they reaped exactly what they sowed and were instantly destroyed by God's Spirit.

We all wonder how this could happen. As I was praying about this, God gave me further revelation. In Genesis, it speaks about the fact that we're made in God's image. Remember He breathed the breath of life into that image, which was man. In other words, the breath of God is sustaining all people. The breath is backed by His creative power.

Now let's think about what was happening in the Church at that time. Great power, great grace and signs and wonders were all being backed by the creative power of God that had been *breathed* through the apostles.

The model that God's glory provides is one of weightiness and increase. There is nothing lacking about God. His glory is a paradigm of His nature. As His children, we should reflect that same abundance by reflecting His glory and by sowing glory into His kingdom.

But we should also be ever mindful of the awesome power that is released in the glory of God.

You cannot separate giving and glory. If I'm a container of God's glory and you sow seed into my ministry, then when I go to Africa and pour out the glory and anointing upon those people, *your seed becomes glory.*

It helps to transform lives and touch people with the power of God.

On the other hand, when a person gives his money to Satan, he sows death and touches others with the power of death. For instance, when a person buys pornography, he is essentially paying someone to go out and seduce young people into compromising their bodies to satisfy that lust. In this manner, their material wealth is creating a chain reaction of wicked deeds. What do they reap? People who spend money like this are sowing death and destruction and reaping the same.

But if it so obviously works in the realm of darkness, then why wouldn't it work in the realm of light? Why not start a chain reaction of God's power? When you sow for God's glory the reward is eternal.

Your seed assists His weightiness in touching all those thousands of people and bringing them life.

What will you reap? You will reap the weightiness of God. When you sow seed, you're sowing glory. When you sow glory, you'll reap glory. You'll reap all that you need for the blessings of God to come to you and upon you.

God earnestly desires to pour His favor all over you and ooze right out of your body so that when you walk out, the blessings of God will just come to you.

That is what He will do in order for you to reap the harvest that you need to reap.

A Vision of God's Weightiness in Action

In conclusion, I believe that Chapters 8 and 9 of Second Corinthians shows a clear correlation and relationship between the blessings of glory and grace concerning giving and receiving! In verses 1 and 2, we can see clearly how they abounded in the riches of their liberality.

This was the result of grace (the Divine influence upon the heart and it's reflection in the life).

For the weightiness of God to grow in your life, grace must continually abound. That's why partaking of grace is so important. It was the result of grace (verse 11 of Chapter 8) that resulted in their readiness and desire to give. We see once again that God delights in a willing heart.

That is why I thought it necessary to urge these brethren to go to you before I do and make arrangements in advance for this bountiful, promised gift of yours, so that it may be ready, not as an extortion [wrung out of you] but as a generous and willing gift.

[Remember] this: he who sows sparingly and grudgingly will also reap sparingly and grudgingly, and he who sows generously [that blessings may come to someone] will also reap generously and with blessings.

Let each one [give] as he has made up his own mind and purposed in his heart, not reluctantly or sorrowfully or under compulsion, for God loves (He takes pleasure in, prizes above other things, and is unwilling to abandon or do without) a cheerful (joyous "prompt to do it") giver [whose heart is in his giving]. [Proverbs 22:9.]

And God is able to make all grace (every favor and earthly blessing) come to you in abundance, so that you may always and under all circumstances and whatever the need be self-sufficient [possessing enough to require no aid or support and furnished in abundance for every good work and charitable donation].

2 Corinthians 9:5-8

Note that partaking of grace and sharing in another's ministry (Philippians 1:7, 4:19) will bring abundance to sow more seeds and bless more ministries.

And they yearn for you while they pray for you, because of the surpassing measure of God's grace (His favor and mercy and spiritual blessing which is shown forth) in you.

Now thanks be to God for His Gift, [precious] beyond telling [His indescribable, inexpressible, free Gift]!

2 Corinthians 9:14,15 (AMP)

Once again, Paul thanks God for his Divine influence that's in *them;* and as a result of that influence, he's in the position of thanking them for their weighty gift.

This kind of *willing heart* that's *anointed to give* creates room for God to bring forth the weightiness of his power that's in your heart and create a weightiness of wealth that will overwhelm you. The giving out of *natural weightiness,* creates a vacuum for the supernatural weightiness of God to fill. It draws God's weightiness to your life. When you sow seeds of glory out of yourself, it creates more room for the influence of glory to come in to your heart and draw to you the wealth of the wicked that's been laid up for the just...namely us.

I encourage you to partake of the blessings of Abraham that came through his absolute obedience.

God is going to get weightier!

The Vision of Sword Ministries

The foundation of this ministry rests in Hebrews 4:12 which is summarized in the following statement, "Speaking the Truth in Revival, Piercing the Innermost Being." We are to remain carriers of revival, "Demonstrating Signs and Wonders, Decently and In Order, by the Power of the Holy Spirit."

Our vision is to see the stadiums of America and around the world filled to capacity in which the fullness of the Gospel of Christ, the Anointed One is declared unto salvation. Not just in persuasive words of man's wisdom, but in demonstration of the Spirit and in Power (Acts 2), which includes salvation according to Acts 10:44.

To see multitudes touched by the loving presentation of the power of God through power packed spirit filled books published in many different languages, world wide multi-media television and radio productions, and churches and Bible schools established in China and other nations, via Apostolic teams and multi-faceted Evangelistic operations.